Gone With The Tide

The Vanishing Gullahs and Geechees

Pearce W. Hammond

Gone With The Tide
The Vanishing Gullahs and Geechees

ISBN-13: 978-1491078495
ISBN-10: 1491078499

Cover Photo and Design
by Pearce W. Hammond

Illustrated with Original Art
by Pearce W. Hammond

Published in the United States by
High Tide Publishing
20 Bellinger Cove
Okatie, South Carolina 29909

This book is dedicated to
Nellie B. Brown

Nellie B. Brown with the Author in 1941.

Table of Contents

INTRODUCTION

In the almost 100 years separting the Civil War and the 1950's, the Lowcountry of South Carolina and Georgia was a world unto itself. The big plantations were gone and for the remaining residents, life had to be wrenched from the soil and the creeks and rivers. But for some, the isolated barrier sea islands of South Carolina and Georgia offered heaven on earth: virgin maritime forests; pristine saltwater; sand roads and wild game. It was life in a simpler time, of raising hogs, chickens and children on abandoned plantations; growing sweet potatoes, okra and sugar cane; trapping wild game; gathering oysters; casting for shrimp; catching a 10-pound flounder or a 65-pound drum from the creeks; catching a bushel basket of Blue Crabs; and making a feast of fish, crabs and oysters.

When I was a young boy in the early 1950's, I spent many weekends with my grandparents at Grove Point Plantation outside of Savannah, Georgia and I was fascinated by the Gullah/Geechee language which was spoken by Lem and Sarah, the African American couple who worked for them and lived at Grove Point.

When I was older, I went on a fishing trip with my father and several of his friends to one of the remote barrier sea islands off the coast of Georgia. We left Savannah and traveled down the Intercoastal Waterway to Blackbeard Island where we anchored behind the island in the mouth of Cabretta Inlet to go surf fishing. On the way there we stopped at Raccoon Bluff, a small Geechee fishing village on Sapelo Island. When we arrived, I felt like I was in an African village. The Geechee people there were very friendly and you could tell that they were cut off from the outside world. They lived off the land and the water and were almost completely self-sufficient and did not have to depend on others for their food and other needs. While we were there, we were invited to share some smoked Mullet and during the meal they spoke their unique Geechee language which I found difficult to understand.

Another experience I had with the Gullah people was when I went duck hunting with my father in the late 1950's at Rose Hill Plantation in Yemassee, South Carolina. When we arrived at the hunting lodge, we were greeted by two Gullah women, Bella and Essie, who prepared all of the meals for the duck hunters on a wood stove and picked all the ducks which were killed each day. While they were in the kitchen cooking and later serving a meal, they sang songs in Gullah. While I was there, one of the hunters celebrated a Birthday and I can still hear Bella and Essie singing as they brought the birthday cake to the table, *"Hoppy, Hoppy, Bird-day, Mr. Jak."*

Then there was an elderly Gullah man, Ely, who arrived each morning around 4 am to build a fire in each room as there was no other source of heat at the hunting lodge. Ely's second job was to transport the hunters and their dogs and decoys to their duck blinds in the old rice fields on the Combahee River before sunrise. Again, I was fascinated with the Gullah language spoken by Ely.

Each of these experiences helped to spark my interest in learning more about the Geechee/Geechee people and their unique language and culture. It is my hope that this book will help to keep their story alive for future generations.

Pearce W. Hammond, Author

The Gullah/Geechee People

Many Americans are unaware that east of I-95 and along the South Carolina and Georgia Coast lies a culture more strongly rooted in African ways than any other in America. In the carolinas the culture is known as "Gullah", and in Georgia, it is known as "Geechee".

The Gullah and Geechee trace their roots to the first slaves arriving in the lowcountry in the early 17th Century and settling on isolated Sea Islands in the lowcountry region of South Carolina and Georgia. This includes both the coastal plain and the Sea Islands. Historically, the Gullah region extended from the Cape Fear area of the coast of North Carolina south to the vicinity of Jacksonville on the coast of Florida.

These islanders brought with them their ancestors' ability to cultivate rice along with many other traditional skills such as farming, basket weaving, net making, fishing, language, pottery, woodcarvings and more.

Along the lush sea islands and the Atlantic coastal plains of the southern East Coast of America, a distinctive group of tidewater communities stuck together throughout the centuries preserving its African cultural heritage and carving out a lifestyle that is uniquely its own.

They lived in small farming and fishing communities and the climate and geographic isolation of the sea islands were integral to the development of their unique culture.

The name "Geechee" may have come from Kissi *(pronounced "Geezee")*, a tribe living in the border area between Guinea, Sierra Leone, and Liberia. Some scholars speculate the name Geechee is related to the Ogeechee River near Savannah, Georgia.

The name "Gullah" may derive from Angola, a country in

southwestern Africa where many of the Gullahs' ancestors originated. Some scholars have also suggested it comes from Gola, an ethnic group living on the border area between Sierra Leone and Liberia in Western Africa.

Most of the Gullahs' ancestors were brought to South Carolina through the port of Charleston, which was one of the most important ports in North America for the Atlantic Slave Trade. Almost half of the enslaved Africans came through the port of Charleston.

Because of geography, climate, and patterns of importation of enslaved Africans, the Gullahs and Geechees are known for preserving more of their African linguistic and cultural heritage than any other African-American community in the United States.

Gullah is a culture unlike any other in the world. It is a

manner of living, working, story telling and beliefs. These original African immigrants were the primary builders of the lucrative rice trade of early colonial America. The skills they had utilized while developing a flourishing culture in Sierra Leone and other Western African countries gave them the know how to adapt these agricultural talents to the marshlands of coastal South Carolina and Georgia. African farmers from the "Rice Coast" brought with them skills for rice cultivation and the rice industry became successful.

In the late 1600s, the Sea Islands of South Carolina, Georgia and northern Florida were covered with thousands of acres of indigo, rice, and cotton plantations. While there were many native Americans and Chinese slaves working on the plantations, as well as European indentured servants, the majority of the workforce consisted of African slaves. Malaria and yellow fever kept many plantation owners away from the  lowcountry leaving their black overseers in charge. The isolation from the mainland and little contact with whites fostered an environment where they developed a culture unique to America.

After the Civil War ended in 1865, and after the abolition of slavery, the slaves were freed and the plantations closed. They then settled in remote villages around the coastal sea islands, where, thanks to their relative isolation, they formed strong communal ties and a unique culture that has endured for centuries.

In quiet self-sufficiency, the Gullahs and Geechees lived off the water and the land in these small farming and fishing communities on the remote sea islands of South Carolina and Georgia and their unique culture thrived in isolation for centuries until the outside world discovered the islands and started paying millions to own them.

Since the 1950's, their farms, their fishing holes and the sea grass fields that fueled their artisty have fallen victim to bulldozers and their land forfeited because landowners, many of whom are domestic workers at the sea island resorts, could not afford to pay the escalating property taxes.

Other traces of the culture, such as cooking, medicines and story telling are increasingly harder to find, and their unique language, a melodic blend of 17th and 18th century

English and African dialects, is rarely spoken today.

If the culture dies, Gullah and Geechee children will not know about the old lifestyle and a significant part of the culture of the low country of South Carolina and Georgia will be lost along with African Americans' purest link to their past.

In many ways the Gullahs and Geechees are part of the modern world and have cars, big-screen televisions and cellular phones. In other ways, they have preserved the traditions of their ancestors.

Estimates about the current number of Gullah and Geechee people vary and exact figures are hard to verify. Some say there are over one million while others estimate the number is closer to 250,000.

To help prevent their extinction, the Gullah/Geechee Cultural Preservation Act was signed into law in October 2006. The Act establishes a "Cultural Heritage Corridor" which extends from Wilmington, North Carolina to Jacksonville, Florida. The U.S. National Park Service will administer the project with strong input from the Gullah / Geechee community.

The bill authorizes $1 million per year for ten years to carry out the work of the commission and calls for one or more interpretive centers within the Cultural Heritage Corridor.

This Act will help to save the Gullah and Geechee culture from extinction and is a long overdue salute to these descendants of slaves who made significant contributions to America's heritage.

To this day, the Gullah and Geechee people are trying to hold steadfastly to the way of life of their African ancestors, passing on their traditons from one generation to another.

Cultural Heritage Corridor

Stretching along the Atlantic Coast is a long line of Sea Islands, some of which are large and some quite small, live African Americans who call themselves Gullah and Geechee and speak a unique language. They are the descendants of slaves who toiled in the island fields and who stayed after Emancipation to become land owners, farmers, teachers, nurses, blacksmiths, doctors and fishermen.

In 2006 the U.S. Congress passed the "Gullah/Geechee Cultural Heritage Corridor Act " that provides $10 million over ten years for the preservation and interpretation of historic sites relating to Gullah/Geechee culture.

The "Cultural Heritage Corridor" will extend from Jacksonville, Florida to Wilmington, North Carolina and the project will be administered by the U.S. National Park Service with strong input from the Gullah/Geechee community.

Sea Islands

The sea islands off the coast of South Carolina and Georgia, have provided Gullah/Geechee roots to millions of African Americans.

The sea islands are a chain of tidal and barrier islands on the Southeastern Atlantic Ocean coast of the United States. They number over 100 and are located between the mouths of the Santee and St. Johns Rivers along the coast of the U.S. States of South Carolina, Georgia and Florida.

Settled by indigenous cultures for thousands of years, the islands were an early site of Spanish founding of colonial missions. Historically the Spanish influenced the Guale and Mocama chiefdoms by establishing missions in their major settlements, from St. Catherine's Island south to Fort George Island *(at present day Jacksonville, Florida)*. Both chiefdoms extended to the coastal areas of the mainland. The Mocama Province included territory to the St. Johns River in present-day Florida. The system ended under pressure of repeated raids by English South Carolina colonists and Indian allies. Spain ceded its territory of Florida to Great Britain in 1763 following the British victory against the French in the Seven Years War.

After 18th-century European-American settlement of

Georgia and Florida, planters imported enslaved Africans as laborers. Many were used to work the labor-intensive cotton, rice and indigo plantations on the Sea Islands. The slaves developed the notable and distinct Gullah/Geechee Creole culture and language which has survived to contemporary times. The islands now are known for resort, recreational, and residential development.

Major Sea Islands

South Carolina Sea Islands

Bull Island, Dewees Island, Edisto Island, Folly Island, Isle of Palms, James Island, Johns Island, Kiawah Island, Morris Island, Seabrook Island, Sullivan's Island, Wadmalaw Island, Bear Island, Bay Point Island, Cane Island, Cat Island, Coosaw Island, Dataw Island, Fripp Island, Gibbes Island, Harbor Island, Hilton Head Island, Parris Island, Port Royal Island, Pritchards Island, St. Helena Island, St. Phillips Island, Spring Island, Daufuskie Island, Distant Island, Hunting Island, Lady's Island, and Morgan Island.

Georgia Sea Islands

Tybee Island, Little Tybee Island, Cockspur Island, Wilmington Island, Talahi Island, Whitemarsh Island, Oatland Island, Skidaway Island, Isle of Hope, Dutch Island, Burnside Island, Wassaw Island, Ossabaw Island, St. Catherine's Island, Isle of Wight, Hampton Island, Blackbeard Island, Sapelo Island, Jekyll Island, Little St. Simons Island, St. Simons Island, Sea Island, Cumberland Island.

Florida Sea Islands

Amelia Island and Fernandina Beach

Gullah/Geechee Language

Forbidden by plantation owners to speak their own native tongue, the African slaves developed their own dialect out of necessity by incorporating broken English with African words. The Gullah/Geechee language is not Black English, nor is it a dialect of any other language. It is a melodic blend of 17th and 18th century English and African dialects and was first spoken by slaves. It is a legitimate creole language with its own grammar, phonological system, idiomatic expressions and an extensive vocabulary. It is one of six languages known as the English-derived Atlantic Creoles and is the only one spoken on the U.S. mainland today. It is estimated that about 200,000 Afro-Americans, descendants of the slaves, who live in the low country of South Carolina and Georgia, still speak Gullah/Geechee. Many of these people live in Charleston and on nearby sea islands.

The Gullah/Geechee dialect survives today as a "creolized" version of English. The Gullah/Geechee language attained creole status during the mid 1700s and was learned and used by the second generation of African Americans as their mother tonque. Growing from African roots, planted in American soil, and nourished by various English dialects, a linguistic analysis of the Gullah language will determine that the greater part of its lexicon is traceable to English words. However, the sentence structure, intonation, and stress reveal a clear correspondence to the languages spoken on the west coast of Africa.

Since Gullah/Geechee is an English-derived creole, the English alphabet is used to represent its sounds. Most of the letters used in the spelling of Gullah/Geechee words have the same sounds that are used to form English words.

Properly referred to as "Sea Island Creole," the Gullah/ Geechee language is related to Jamaican Patois, Barbadian Dialect, Bahamian Dialect, Belizean Creole and the Krio language of Sierra Leone in West Africa. It is strongly influenced by West African languages such as Vai, Mende, Twi, Ewe, Hausa, Yoruba, Igbo and Kikongo.

Since the late 19th century, various experts on Gullah have speculated that the language might die within the next generation because it allegedly had fewer and fewer native speakers, especially among the young. However, once one realizes that there was never a time in American history when Gullah was spoken by every coastal African American, there may not be much reason to fear that its potential death may be imminent. Although there were several migrations out of the Sea Islands region during the 20th century, predominantly to escape poverty, many of those who left have returned, often quite disenchanted with life in the city and eager to hold on to their heritage language as a marker of cultural identity. Gullah storytelling, cuisine, music, folk beliefs, crafts, farming and fishing traditions all exhibit strong influences from West and Central African cultures. Gullah is a legitimate creole language and one that should be preserved as a significant part of our American heritage. The Gullah/Geechee language is helping record and document a fascinating part of America's heritage.

The following examples highlights some
of the differences between Gullah and English:

"Hah hunnuh fah do"? - Translation: How are you?

"Hunnuh mus tek cyear ahde root fah heal de tree"! - Translation: You have to take care of the roots in order to heal the tree!

"Ef hunnuh ain kno weh hunnuh da from, hunnuh ain gwine kno weh hunnuh dey gwine"! - Translation: If you don't know where you are from, you won't know where you are going!

"Bwoy hunnuh betta cumyah befo mi jux yah"! - Translation: Boy you better come here before I whoop you!

"De Gullah gone a plowin een de fiel e fambly own and gone home tyad to de bone, bot him been good en glad." - Translation: The Gullah went plowing in the field his family owns and went home very tired but very glad.

"Uh wu'k tell uh agonize me bone" - Translation: I have worked until I am exhausted.

"Uh kin dribe de auttymobile?" - Translation: May I drive the automobile?

"Two 'ooman git bactize." - Translation: Two women were baptized.

"Drap de aig een bilin' watuh." - Translation: Drop the eggs in boiling water.

"De fench mek ub boa'd." - Translation: The fence is made of boards.

"Bofe de mens wu'k." - Translation: Both men worked.

"Pa bress de bittle." - Translation: Father blessed the food.

"Dat gal hab uh bush-chile." - Translation: That girl has an illegitimate child.

"Ma mek cawncake fuh suppuh." - Translation: Mother made cornbread for supper.

"De gal, dem, gone wu'k duh de cawnfiel." - Translation: The girl and the others went to work in the cornfield.

"Daa'tuh cook two chickin fuh dinnuh." - Translation: Daughter cooked two chickens for dinner.

"Sandy Claw come down de chimbly." - Translation: Santa Claus came down the chimney.

"Daa'tuh gone sto'." - Translation: Daughter went to the store.

"De chile foot col'." - Translation: The Child's feet are cold.

"De watuh cyaam; us gwi' cas' de net." - Translation: The water is calm; we're going to cast the net.

"De leetle gal cyan' tote de baby." - Translation: The little girl can't carry the baby.

"Dat gal ent study wu'k; 'e too lub fuh flash-'bout." - Translation: That girl doesn't think about work; she likes to have fun.

"fo'" - Translation: I made four dollars.

"E bayre feet." - Translation: He is barefooted.

"Ma hab fo'teen chillun." - Translation: Mother had fourteen children.

"dese" - Translation: These are Mother's chickens.

The Lord's Prayer in Gullah/Geechee

We Fada wa dey een heaben,
leh ebrybody hona ya name.
We pray dat soon ya gwine
rule oba de wol,
wasoneba ting ya wahn,
leh um be so een dis wol
same like dey een heaben.
Gii we de food wa we need
dis day yah an ebry day.
Fagib we fa we sin,
same like we da fagib
dem people wa do bad ta we.
Leh we dohn hab haad test
wen Satan try we.
Keep we from ebil.

The New Testament *(De Nyew Testament)* in Gullah Sea Island Creole with marginal text of the King James Version was completed after 26 years of translating and was introduced at the Heritage Days Festival on St. Helena Island, SC, on November 12, 2005.

"Fa de fus time, God taak to me de way I taak."

Translation: For the first time, God talks to me the way I talk.

29

Gullah/Geechee Words

Abnue - avenue.
Agg - egg.
An - and.
arter - after.
Arur - each, either.
Ax - ask
Bactize - baptize.
Bague - to beg.
Barruh - barrow.
Beber - beaver.
Bedout - without.
Ben - bend, bent, been.
Berry - very.
Bes - best.
Bex - vex, vexed.
Bidness - business.
Biggin - begin, began.
Bimeby - by and by, presently.
Binner - was, were.
Bittle - victuals.
Blan - in the habit of, accustomed to.
Blanks - belongs to.
Bleebe - believe.
Bieege - obliged, compelled.
Bodder - to bother.
Bode - board, boards.
Bofe - both.
Bole - bold.
Boun - resolved upon,forced to.
Bredder - brother.
Bref - breath.
Bres - breast.
Bresh - brush-wood, to brush.
Broke up - to leave, to depart.
Brukwus - breakfast.
Buckra - white man.
Bud - bird.

Budduh - brother.
Bun - burn.
Buss - burst, or break through.

Cahr - carry.
Caze - because.
Ceive - deceive.
Cept - accept, accepted, except.
Chillun - children.
Chimbly - chimmey.
Chune - tune.
Cist - insist.
Clorte - cloth.
Cloze - clothes.
Cohoot - bargain, agreement.
Cole - cold.
Conjunct - agree to, conclude.
Cote - court.
Crack eh teet - make answer.
Crap - crop.
Crape - scrape.
Cratch - scratch.
Cut down - disappointed, chagrined.

Darter - daughter.
Day - there, is, to be, am.
Day day - to be there.
Den - then
Der - was, were, into.
Dest - just, only.
Destant - distant, distance.
Det - death.
Diffunce - difference.
Disher - this.
Do - door.
Dout - without.
Drap - drop, dropped.
Duh - was, were.

Dunno - don't know.
Dut - dirt.
Edder - other.
Eeben - even.
Een - in, end.
Eenwite - invite.
Ef - if.
Eh - he, she, it, his, her, its.

Faber - favor.
Faid - to be afraid.
Fambly - family.
Fanner - a shallow basket.
Farruh, Farrur - father.
Feber - fever
Fedder - feather, feathers.
Fiel - field
Fine - supply with food, find.
Flaber - flavor.
Flo - floor.
Flut - flirt.
Foce - force.
Forrud - forehead.
Fren - friend.
Fros - frost.
Fuh - for.
Fuh sutten - for a certainty.
Fuss - first.

Gage - engage.
Gedder - gather, collect.
Gelt - to girt.
Gem - to give.
Gen - gave, again.
Gie - give.
Gimme - give me.
Glec - neglect.

Glub - gloves.
Gooly - good.
Graff - grab.
Gree - agree, consent.
Grine salt - fly round and round.
Guine, Gwine - going, going to.

Haffer - have to, had to.
Hair rise - badly frightened.
Haky, Harky - hearken to, heed.
Han - hand.
Hanker - long for, desire.
Hatchich - hatchet.
Head - get the better of.
Head um - get ahead of him.
Hebby - heavy.
Holler - halloo, hollow.
Honna - you.
Hot - to hurt.
Huccum - how happens it, why,
          how come.
Huddy - how d 'ye do.
Ile me bade - grease my mouth.
Isself - himself, herself, itself,
          themselves.
Jew - dew.
Jist - just.
Juk - jerk.
Ketch - catch, reach to, approach.
Kibber - cover.
Kine - kind.
Knowledge - acknowledge, admit.
Labuh - labor.
Lass - to suffice for, to last.
Lean fuh - set out for.
Led - dow - lay down.
Leek - to lick with the tongue.

Leely, Leetle - little.
Leff - to leave, did leave, left.
Leggo - to let go.
Leh - let.
Lemme - let me.
Lenk - length.
Libbin - living.
Lick - to whip, stroke of the whip.
Lickin - whipping.
Lick back - turn rapidly back.
Lief - leave, permission.
Light on - to mount.
Light out - to start off.
Long - with, from.
Lub - love.
Luk, lucker - like.
Mange - mane.
Medjuh - measure.
Mek - Make, made.
Mek fuh - to go to.
Mek out - fare, thrive, succeed.
Member - to remind.
Men eh pace - increase his speed.
Mine - mind, heed, take care of.
Miration - wonder, astonishment.
Mo - more.
Moober - moreover.
Mona, moner - more than.
Most - almost.
Mossa - master.
Mouf, Mout - mouth.
Murrer - mother.
Mussne - must not.
Muster - must have.
Nabor - neighbor.
Narruh - another.
Nebber - never.
Nekked - naked.

Nigh - to draw near to.
Notus - notice, observe.
Noung - young.
Nudder - another.
Nuff - enough.
Nummine - never mind.
Nurrer - neither, another.
Nuse - use, employ.
Nussen - used to, accustomed to.
Nuss - nurse.
Nuttne - nothing.
Obersheer - overseer.
Offer - off of.
Ole - old.
Ooman - woman, women.
Out - to go out, to extinguish.
Outer - out of.
Pahler - parlor.
Passon - parson.
Pate - path.
Pen pon - depend upon.
Perwision - provisions.
Pinder - ground-nuts, peanuts.
Pint - direct, directed, point.
Pintment - appointment.
Pit - put, apply.
Playpossum - to fool, to practice
                deceit.
Pledjuh - pleasure.
Po - poor, pour.
Pon, upon.
Pooty, pretty.
Pose, post.
Prommus - promise.
Pruppus - on purpose.
Pusson - person.
Quaintun - acquainted with.
Quaintunce - acquaintances.

Quile - to coil, coiled.
Quire - to inquire, inquired.
Rale - very, truly, really.
Range - reins.
Rastle - to wrestle.
Retch - to reach, to arrive at.
Ribber - river.
Riz - rose.
Roose - roost.
Sabe - to know.
San - sand.
Sarbis - service, kindness.
Satify - satisfied, content, happy.
Scace - scarce.
Schway - to swear, swore.
Scuse - excuse.
Seaznin - seasoning.
Sebbn - seven
Sed - sit, sat.
Sed-down - sit down, sat down.
Shet - shut.
Sho - sure.
Sholy - surely.
Shum - to see it, see him, see her, see them.
Sider - on the side of.
Sisso - say so.
Skade - scared.
Smate - smart.
Sofe - soft.
Soon man - very smart, wide-awake man.

Sorter - sort of, after a fashion.
Sparruh - sparrow.
Spec - expect.
Spose - expose.
Spute - contest the championship
         with.
State - start, begin.

Steader, Stidder - instead of.
Straighten fur - run rapidly for.
Stroy - destroy.
Sukkle - circle, fly around.
Summuch - so much.
Sutten - certain, sudden.
Suttenly - certainly, suddenly.
Swade, persuade.
Swode - sword.
Tack - to attack.
Tackie - to hold to account.
Tan - to stand.
Tarrify - to terrify, to annoy.
Tarruh, Turruh - the other.
Tase - to taste, taste.
Tay - stay.
Tek - take.
Tek you foot - to walk.
Tel - until.
Ten - attend to.
Tend - intend.
Tenk, Tenky - to thank, thanks.
Tetch - to touch.
Tetter - potatoes.
Tick - thick, abundant, a stick.
Ticket - thicket.
Tickler - particular.
Tief - to steal, thief.
Ting - thing.
Tird - third.
Titter - sister.
Togerruh - together.
Tole - Told
Topper - on top of, on.
Tote - carry.
Trabble - travel.
Tru - through.
Truss - trust.

Trute - truth.
Tuff - tuft.
Tuk - took.
Tun - turn, return.
Tun flour - to cook hominy.
Up ter de notch - in the best style.
Usen - to be in the habit of.
Vise - to advise.
Vive - revive.
Wan - to want, to wish, want.
Warse - wasp.
Wase - waste.
Way - where.
Wayebber - wherever.
Whalin ob er - enormous, severe.
Wid - with.
Wile - while.
Win - Wind.
Wine - vine.
Wish de time er day - to say goodby,
how d 'ye do.
Wud - word.
Wudduh dat - what is that.
Wuffer - what for, why, what to.
Wuh - what, which,who.
Wuhebber -whatever.
Wuk - work.
Wul - world.
Wunt - will not, would not.
Wurrum - worms.
Wus - worse.
Wus den nebber - worse than ever.
Wut, worth.

Yad, yard.
Yearin - hearing.
Yeddy - to hear, to hearken to.

. Yent day day - is not there, are not there.
Yeye - eye, eyes.
Yez - ear, ears.
Yiz - am, is, to be, did.
Yuh - here.
Zamine - examine.

NUMBERS
One - one.
Two - two.
Tree - three.
Fo - four.
Fibe - five.
Six - six.
Sebbn - seven.
Eight - eight.
Nine - nine.
Ten - ten.
Lebbn - eleven.
Twelbe - twelve.
Tirteen - thirteen.
Foteen - fourteen.
Fifteen - fifteen.
Sixteen - sisteen.
Sebbnteen - seventeen.
Eighteen - eighteen.
Nineteen - nineteen.
Twenty - twenty.
Tirty - thirty.
Forty - forty.
Fifty - fifty.
Sixty - sixty.
Sebbnty - seventy.
Eighty - eighty.
Ninety - ninety.
One hundud - one hundred.
One tousan - one thousand.

MONTHS OF THE YEAR

Jinnywerry - January.
Febbywerry - February.
Mache - March.
Aprul - April.
May - May.
June - June.
Jully - July.
Augus - August.
Sectember - September.
October - October.
November - November.
December - December.

DAYS OF THE WEEK

Mundy - Monday.
Chuseday - Tuesday.
Wensday - Wednesday.
Tursday - Thursday.
Friday - Friday.
Sattyday - Saturday.
Sunday - Sunday.

Low Country Spirituals

Swing Low, Sweet Cha'iot

Swing low, sweet cha'iot,
Comin' fuh tuh cyaa' me home.
Swing low, sweet cha'iot
Comin' fuh tuh cyaa' me home.

Uh look obuh Jerding en' w'at I see
Comin' fuh tuh cyaa' me home.
A ban'ob ainjul comin' attuh me,
Comin' fuh tuh cyaa' me home.

Uh look obuh Jerding en' w'at I see
Comin' fuh tuh cyaa' me home.
A cha'iot ob fiah wid uh ainjul dribuh,
Comin' fuh tuh cyaa' me home.

I'se sometime up en' sometime down,
Comin' fuh tuh cyaa' me home.
En' Uh still my soul wid a heb' (m)ly powuh,
Comin' fuh tuh cyaa' me home.

BURDING DOWN

Burding down, burding down
W'en I lay my burding down
Burding down, burding down
W'en I lay my burding down.

Who is dis one dress een red?
W'en I lay my burding down.
Mus' be duh chillun Mosey led
W'en I lay my bvurding down.

Who is dis one dress een w'ite?
W'en I lay my burding down
Mus' be duh chillun ob duh Isr'alite
W'en I lay my burding down.

DUH GOLDING RIBBUH

W'en I cross duh golding Ribbuh
  Don'chuh grieb' attuh me,
W'en I cross duh golding Ribbuh
  Don'chuh grieb' attuh me.
W'en I cross duh golding Ribbuh
  Don'shuh grieb' attuh me.
Oh, I do(n)' wan'chuh fuh grieb' attuh me.

W'en yuh yeddy dem wing-a-rustlin',
  Don'chuh grieb' attuh me,
W'en yuh yeddy dem wing a-rustlin',
  Don'chuh grieb' attuh me.
W'en yuh yeddy dem wing-a-rustlin,
  Don'shuh grieb' attuh me.
Oh, I do(n)' wan'chuh fuh grieb' attuh me.

EB'RYBAWDY WHO IS LIBBIN' GAWT'UH DIE

Eb'rybawdy who is libbin' gawt'uh die, gawt'uh die,
Eb'rybawdy who is libbin' gawt'uh die, gawt'uh die,
Duh rich en' duh po', duh great en' duh small,
All gawt'uh meet at duh jedgement hall,
Eb'rybawdy who is libbin' gawt'uh die, gawt'uh die,

Eb'rybawdy who is libbin' gawt'uh die, gawt'uh die,
Eb'rybawdy who is libbin' gawt'uh die, gawt'uh die,
Duh n'yung en' duh ole, duh shawt en' duh tall,
All gawt'uh meet at duh jedgement hall,
Eb'rybawdy who is libbin' gawt'uh die.

Eb'ry deacon who is libbin' gawt'uh die, gawt'uh die,
Eb'ry deacon who is libbin' gawt'uh die, gawt'uh die,
Duh n' yung en duh ole, duh shawt en' duh tall,
All gawt'uh meet at duh jedgement hall,
Eb'rybawdy who is libbin' gawt'uh die, gawt'uh die,

The Bahamian
Connection

Culturally and linguistically, the character and personality of the Bahamian people owe much to the Gullah and Geechee people who live on the coastal islands of South Carolina and Georgia.

Today, the English spoken by the average working class Bahamian is close to the Gullah and Geechee dialect, so much so, that Bahamian migrant workers who found their way to the American South as farm workers on *"The Contract"*, during and after World War II, could melt into the local population because they could speak Gullah and Geechee. Idioms like *'day clean'* for dawn and *'terectly'* for *"soon"* or *"whenever"* are still commonly used in both Charleston and Nassau.

The slaves in the Bahamas and the Caribbean were freed in 1834 by Queen Victoria. By that time, all Bahamians of African descent, whether they arrived with the Loyalists or whether they preceeded the loyalists, or whether they arrived by other means, were influenced by the culture and folkways of the Gullah and Geechee people.

In 1718, the islands became a British Crown colony, and the first Royal Governor, a reformed pirate named Woodes Rogers, expelled the Buccaneers who had used the islands as hideouts. During the American War of Independence the Bahamas fell briefly to Spanish forces under General Galvez in 1782.

After the American Revolutionary War, the British government issued land grants in Jamaica, Canada and the Bahamas to a group of British Loyalists, who chose the wrong side in the war. The sparse population of the Bahamas tripled in a few years. The planters thought to grow cotton, but the limestone soil, the boll weevil and chenille bug put an end to those dreams. After a few years, the plantations failed and soon both the Black and White settlers turned to the sea for their fortunes.

The cultures of the Bahamian and the American South also share a great story-telling tradition, and many of the themes and motifs suggest a common African past. But what is remarkable is that researchers have found one of the largest collections of folk-tales in the hemisphere in The Bahamas, over three hundred or more, and only in Africa are more folk-tales found and still told today. These stories speak to an African origin, particularly the Anansi stories, and show a commonality wherever Africans were settled in the new world.

Traditionally, parents and grandparents in the Bahamas, drew on B' Booky and B'Rabby folk tales to put their children to sleep. These folk-tales have much in common with the Uncle Remus stories collected over a hundred years ago by a white Southerner, Joel Chandler Harris. The Bahamas however is recognized as having one of the largest collections of folktales in the African Diaspora in the Americas, and their preservation owes much to the work of Zora Neale Hurston, one of the leading figures of the Harlem Renaissance. Hurston is credited with documenting a wide collection of Bahamian folktales, songs and chants that still enrich the Bahamian society today.

For example, in one of his stories, *"How the Alligator Skin Got Wrinkled,"* Harris used the word "Nyam" which means, "to eat." The word is still common in Jamaican dialect and residents of Cat Island and Andros use it to refer to a shoulder bag used for carrying food when going to work in the fields.

Other idioms, which occur in Bahamian dialect, include:

Tell him, say…	-	Tell him
One man	-	A man
Me one	-	Me alone, only me
Mash up	-	Break, hurt, destroy
The headway I make	-	The speed I make
He rig a plan	-	He made a plan
He jook a fish	-	He speared a fish

Religious Traditions

The blending of African and European religions created an energetic and positive mixture that is uniquely Gullah and Geechee. One of the religious traditions which survived well into the twentieth century was "seeking". Seeking combined the European practice of being instructed in the Castechism, a book of questions and answers about the scriptures and Christianity, and the African initiation ceremonies in which the young were required to go into the bush to be instructed by the older members of their tribe.

Making the decision to give your life to the lord was, and still is, taken very seriously by the Gullah and Geechee. Giving your life to the lord meant that you gave up all worldly activity and pleasures and concentrated on being a good Christian.

In the Gullah and Geechee churches, each person was required to go through the lengthy process of seeking before being accepted into the fellowship of a church. The Gullah and Geechee practice of seeking one's soul's salvation was much more involved than in other African-American churches. The seeker in the Gullah and Geechee church began his or her faith walk with a dream or vision. The seeker was matched with a leader, a spiritual teacher, or spiritual mother, who guided the seeker through the seeking experience. Then he or she was required to remove themself from the rest of the world, including family and friends. They spent time alone in meditation and prayer, usually in the backyard or often in the woods at night. The seeker gave up everything while praying. Each evening the seeker told his dream to his spiritual leader who interpreted the dream or vision. You came through your seeking if in your dream, someone gave something to you. This type of dream was interpreted by the spiritual leader to be the gift of the Holy Spirit. When the spiritual teacher is confident that their charge had "come tru" (through), they call all of the elders of the church together to listen to the seeker's dream. If the elders were all satisfied that the seeker's experiences were genuine, the seeker was taught the Catechism to understand their faith. The seeker was then quizzed on his knowledge of the Catechism by the Praise House committee and deacons of the church. If he or she passed, they became a candidate for baptism. If they failed, they went before a tribunal court, consisting of the leader and the committeemen.

The final step of the seeking process occurred when the presider or ward came to the local praise house to lead the worship. The presider or ward was like a Bishop; he was highly respected and revered. Everyone showed up at praise when the presider came. People from neighboring Praise Houses and churches packed the church. They came to celebrate. They sang hymns, spirituals and listened to the presider deliver his sermonette. The period of seeking was long and involved and required prayer, fasting and meditation. The time between seeking *(expressing a desire to seek one's soul's salvation)* and actually "coming tru" *(receiving approval of elders)* could take months.

Seeking was just one of the traditions which survived in the Gullah churches and Praise Houses. Another was the pomp and ceremony of baptisms. Gullah baptisms were frequently held at ebb (low) tide so that the sins of the converts would be taken out with the tide.

Baptisms took place twice a year in May and August. The preacher or leader lead the processional of white-clad  converts and church members from the praise house down to the banks of the nearby creek or river. Songs such as *"All Muh Sins Done Wash Away"* told the story of being baptized at ebb tide. The preacher then took the candidates, one at a time, and dipped them in the creek. Then he prayed that the water would wash their sins away.

After baptism, there was a break to allow the deacons to set up communion. Then the congregation would come together again for the right hand of fellowship which welcomed the new members into the fellowship of that church. After the service, there was a period of singing and shouting.

The "shout" was usually the last part of the praise meeting, often lasting well into the night. The old-fashioned "ring-shout" combined the African traditions of the circle and ring dance with Christian values. During the shouting period, benches were pushed back to the wall, leaving a large open space in the center of the room like a dance hall. The Sea Islanders enjoyed the shout for they believed it "exercised the frame" and was good physical exercise for the body. Shouts were performed as much for entertainment as worship. Today the descendants of the Gullah and Geechee continue to have a spiritual life that influences every aspect of their lives. They believe in the dual nature of the soul and spirit. In death, one's soul returns to God but the spirit remains on earth living among the individual's descendants and participates in their daily affairs such as protecting them and guiding them through spiritual forces.

Living From The Land

Living close to the land has long defined Gullah Culture. They raised their own vegetables, planted their own corn and peas, and ground corn to make flour and grits. They killed hogs and cows for meat and went into the creeks and rivers for fish, crab, shrimp, oysters and clams.

"*My daddy took me in de field and taught me 'bout using a Hoe when I was a little girl. I learned myself how to use dat Hoe and Ise used it tru de years.*"

Gullah farmers hoed the sandy soil to grow vegetables and cotton and for generations the same peaceful way of life continued. It was filled with hard work but also with self- sufficiency and satisfaction.

Among the many plants brought from Africa with the slave trade to the soil of South Carolina and Georgia were Okra, Benneseed, Cowpeas, Watermelon, Eggplant, and Peanuts.

*"De Gullah gone a plowin een de fiel e fambly own.
Fus, e unhitch e hoss from weh hit beenna feedin all
lone. Dat one lee hoss plow up all the dan de
Gullah had. De Gullah gone home tyad to de bone,
bot him been good en glad."*

Translated: "The gullah went plowing in the field
his family owns. First, he unhitched his horse from
where it was feeding all alone. That one small horse
plowed all the land the Gullah had. The Gullah
went home very tired but very glad."

"*I work all de time from morning till late at night and never knowed what it was to rest. I had to do everything there was to do on de outside - work in de field, chop dat wood, hoe dat corn. I done everything except split dem rails.*"

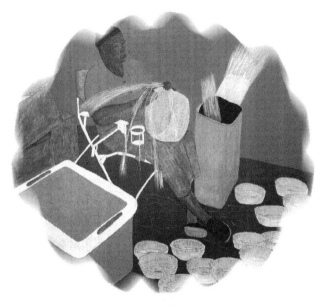

Basket making is one of the nation's oldest art forms of African origin. Sea islanders wove baskets of sweet-smelling, pliable marsh grass to hold vegetables, cotton, shellfish and clothing. Today they make and sell these baskets to supplement their income. The world famous Charleston Sweetgrass basket, a 1000 year old art form, still survives and a visitor to Charleston's Market can watch the basket ladies as they use weaving tools made of bone to preserve this millennium old craft.

Living From The Water

The myriad of waterways that wind
around the sea islands made travel by
boat a necessity for Gullahs and
Geechees from the earliest days of
settlement and the abundance of fish,
crab, shrimp and oysters provided food
as well.

Oystering is a tradition of pride and hard work and for generations Gullah oystermen went out at low tide and harvested bushels of oysters.

Gullah oystermen went out during the "R" months of fall and winter in flat-bottomed wooden boats called "Bateaux" and harvested oysters from the river banks and then transported them back to the oyster factory.

One oysterman could gather 60 to 100 bushels of oysters during a low tide and transport them to the oyster factory where they were steamed, shucked and canned.

Most of the Gullah oystermen who worked the rivers and gathered oysters are now old or dead and their sons and grandsons have taken up other lines of work or have moved away. The Gullah oysterman on the river is nearing an end in our time.

Heavily laden with oysters in his flat bottomed wooden Bateau, a Gullah oysterman heads back to the oyster factory. These boats were rugged and river-worthy and their long wide shape was made to haul enormous loads of oysters.

Gullah oystermen wash down bushels of
oysters on the docks at the oyster factory.

At the oyster factory shovel loads of oysters are heaved onto long cement tables where Gullah/Geechee women use strong hands and small strong-tempered knives to open the shells, remove the oysters, and put them in steel pails. The working tradition of the Gullah/Geechee oystermen and women comes from the river and the tides.

Gullah communities were established on the sea islands by freed slaves after the Civil War. Many of them were fishermen who made their living and provided food for their families fishing the rivers and creeks in the low country.

Gullah/Geechee women pick shrimp caught on the river at low tide.

Bridge Fishing in the low country.

Gullah and Geechee fishermen used their skills on the water to provide food for their families and to prepare traditional recipes such as fried fish, stewed shrimp, oyster dressing, and boiled crabs.

Gullah and Geechee women used hand lines with baskets to catch blue crabs using fish heads, chicken necks and other bait to attract them.

Oysterman on the River

Cleaning Fish For A Fish Fry.

Gullah and Geechee fishermen made their own cast nets and went into the creeks and rivers to catch Shrimp. Throwing a cast net is an acquired skill and learning how to use it was passed down from one generation to another.

Casting for Shrimp on the River.

Gullah Crabbers pulling in a crab trap loaded with Blue Crabs.

Casting for Shrimp at low tide with a cast net. At night he will go out to cast his net for Mullet. When he comes back from the river, he will have enough Shrimp and Mullet to sell and to provide food for his family.

Gullah/Geechee
Superstitions

Here are a few of the many Gullah/GeecheeSuperstitions

1. If bubbles form on top of your coffee, you will get money soon.

2. Rheumatism can be cured by carrying an Irish (white) potato in your pocket.

3. When you hear a screech owl, it's a sure sign of death.

4. Never throw your hair outside because it's a part of your personal body and someone could use it to put a "fix" on you.

5. If a dog howls outside, it's a sign that somebody is dead or dying.

6. It is bad luck to sweep after sundown because you'll sweep yourself out of a home. This superstition may also be based on the African belief that the good spirits come into the house at night and may be swept out by mistake along with the dust.

7. The Gullahs dressed graves with life's necessities and pleasures so the departed could pass easily and amiably between material and spiritual worlds: a cup of water for thirst, a jar of rice for hunger, a lantern for light, a wooden pistol for protection, a bed frame for rest, herbs for health. They regarded cemeteries as sacred ground and left them alone.

8. They painted houses blue to banish evil spirits and tossed salt to get rid of unwanted guests. They also painted some rooms inside blue to keep out spirits, called hags, during childbirth.

9. Long ago a Gullah root doctor might have advised a friend with high blood pressure to tuck a little moss into the shoe sole, or to dress a wound with cobwebs to stop bleeding, or to brew holly berry tea to ease pain.

Gullah Folklore
Hags, Witches and Hants

Hags and Hants are a part of Gullah Folklore. Most folks believe that Hags are witches who live normal lives during the day but at night they shed their skin and go out to "ride" people in their sleep. This means that they sit on the chest of their victims and make them have nightmares. Some say that they suck up the victim's voice so that they can't scream or call out to anyone. A few people claim to have actually touched a Hag. Those who have touched a Hag describe the sensation as "touching warm raw meat." Stories of skin-shedding Hags probably have their beginnings in the West Indies where the people believe that Hags and witches shed their skins after midnight and travel around at will. Another carryover from the West Indies is that the Hag is part witch and part vampire. She can fly and she can suck blood. One old man said: "*Dey goes in en sucks your blood troo yer nose.*" Another superstition is that a Hag won't cross your doorsill if you put a broom across it. Some say that the Hag will not only try to count the straws in the broom, but will also try to measure the length of each one. Therefore, a broom might keep the old Hag too busy to notice that the sun is coming up and she'll get caught. Hags can't stand sunlight or salt so they always leave the victim's house before the sun rises and return to their bodies. Haunts or Hants are more powerful than Hags. As spirits of the dead they can walk right through doors and walls. They are most likely seen when the moon is full and they make strange things happen in the house like lifting the lid of a jar or causing a rocking chair to rock without anyone sitting in it. They will do anything to scare the occupant of the house. Haints are everywhere but they seem to prefer graveyards and swamps.

Customs and Traditions

--**Gullah word "Guber"** for peanut derives straight from Kongo (Congo) word "N'guba"

---**Gullah rice dishes** called "red rice" and "okra soup" are similar to West African "jollof rice" and "okra soup". Jollof rice is a style of cooking brought by the Wolof and Mande peoples of West Africa.

---**The Gullah version of "Gumbo"** has its roots in African cooking. "Gumbo" is derived from a word in the Umbundu language of Angola, meaning "okra."

---**Gullah rice farmers** once used the mortar and pestle and "fanner" *(winnowing basket)* similar to tools used by West African rice farmers.

---**Gullah beliefs about "Hags", "Haunts"** and "plat-eyes" are similar to African beliefs about malevolent ancestors, witches, and "devils" *(forest spirits)*.

---**Gullah "root doctors"** protect their clients against dangerous spiritual forces using similar ritual objects to those employed by African medicine men.

---**Gullah herbal medicines** are similar to traditional African remedies.

---**The Gullah "seekin" ritual** is similar to coming of age ceremonies in West African secret societies like Poro and Sande.

---**Gullah spirituals, shouts,** and other musical forms employ the "call and response" method commonly used in African music.

---**Gullah "sweetgrass baskets"** are almost identical to coil baskets made by the Wolof people in Senegal.

---**The folk song Michael Row the Boat Ashore** *(or Michael Row Your Boat Ashore)* comes from the Gullah culture.

Folk Tales

Brer Lion an Brer Goat

Brer Lion bin a hunt, an eh spy Brer Goat duh leddown topper er big rock duh wuk eh mout an der chaw. Eh creep up fuh ketch um. Wen eh git close ter um eh notus um good. Brer Goat keep on chaw. Brer Lion try fuh fine out wuh Brer Goat duh eat. Eh yent see nuttne nigh um ceptin de nekked rock wuh eh duh leddown on. Brer Lion stonish. Eh wait topper Brer Goat. Brer Goat keep on chaw, an chaw, an chaw. Brer Lion cant mek de ting out, an eh come close, an eh say: "Hay! Brer Goat, wuh you duh eat?" Brer Goat skade wen Brer Lion rise up befo um, but eh keep er bole harte, an eh mek ansur: "Me duh chaw dis rock, an ef you dont leff, wen me done long um me guine eat you." Dis big wud sabe Brer Goat. Bole man git outer diffikelty way coward man lose eh life.

Translation: Brer Lion was hunting, and he spied Brer Goat lying down on top of a big rock working his mouth and chewing. He crept up to catch him. When he got close to him, he watched him good. Brer Goat kept on chewing. Brer Lion tried to find out what Brer Goat was eating. He didn't see anything near him except the naked rock which he was lying down on. Brer Lion was astonished. He waited for Brer Goat. Brer Goat kept on chewing, and chewing, and chewing. Brer Lion couldn't make the thing out, and he came close, and he said: "Hey! Brer Goat, what are you eating?" Brer Goat was scared when Brer Lion rose up before him, but he kept a bold heart, and he made (his) answer: "I am chewing this rock, and if you don't leave me (alone), when I am done with it I will eat you." This big word saved Brer Goat. A bold man gets out of difficulty where a cowardly man loses his life.

Buh Rabbit An De Groun-Mole

Day nebber bin a man wuh kin equel Buh Rabbit fuh mek plan fuh lib offer tarruh people bedout wuk isself. Groun-mole, bin berry tick. On ebry side dem bin er root up de tetter patch, and stroy pinder. No body know how fuh ketch um, case eh wuk onder de groun, and wen you go fuh fine um eh yent dedday.

Buh Rabbit, him see eh chance, an eh tell ebry body him know how fuh stroy um. De ting come ter Buh Wolf yez, an eh sen fuh Buh Rabbit. Buh Rabbit gone ter Buh Wolf, an eh tell um yes, him hab plan fuh clear de fiel er Groun-mole, an dat him wunt charge Buh Wolf nuttne but him boad and lodgment wile him duh ketch an kill de Groun-mole. Buh Wolf, him say Buh Rabbit berry kine,an eh gree fuh fine um. Den Buh Wolf hab one nice bed mek up fuh Buh Rabbit, and eh tell eh wife fuh feed um well.

Buh Wolf hab some bidness wuh call um way from home, an eh spec fuh gone bout one week. Eh leff Buh Rabbit fuh clean de Groun-mole outer eh fiel, an den eh gone. Buh Rabbit, him well saterfy. Ebry mornin, arter brukwus, eh mobe off luk eh bin gwine ter Buh Wolf fiel, an nobody shum tel dinner time. Arter eh done eat er hebby dinner, eh gone gen tel supper time, wen eh come back an eat er hebby supper, an den eh leddown der bed. Nobody kin see any Groun-mole wuh Buh Rabbit der ketch, but eh tell Buh Wolf wife dat eh bin er kill heap er dem ebry day, an dat eh gwine soon clear de fiel. De ting gone on dis way tel Buh Wolf tun home. Wen eh retch eh house eh quire bout Buh Rabbit, an eh wife tell um wuh Buh Rabbit bin er say an er do, an dat Buh Rabbit gone der fiel dist arter brukwus. Buh Wolf say him gwine see fuh ehself wuh Buh Rabbit duh do, an wuh plan eh fix fuh ketch de Groun-mole.

Wen eh git der fiel eh look up an down, an eh yent see no ign er Buh Rabbit. Eh notus eh crap, an de Groun-mole duh eat um wus den nebber. Eh sarche fuh Buh Rabbit track, an eh cant shum no way. Buh Wolf mek up eh mine dat Buh Rabbit yent do de fus ting een de fiel. De sun hot. Buh Wolf gone een de edge er de wood, an day eh come pon topper Buh Rabbit tretch out een er bed wuh eh bin mek outer pine straw onder one tree, fas tersleep. Eh yent bin study bout Buh Wolf, er de Groun-mole wuh bin er bodder de fiel. Buh Wolf slip up, and eh graff um tight. Buh Rabbit so skade eh furgit fuh lie, anBuh Wolf mek um confess eh yent know how fuh ketch Groun-mole, dat eh nebber did kill none, an dat eh bin lib offer Buh Wolf bittle ebber sence eh leff. Buh Wolf, him so be eh git grape wine an eh tie Buh Rabbit han an foot, an eh lick um tel eh tired. All dis time Buh Rabbit bin er holler an er bague. At lenk Buh Wolf loose um, an run um offer de place.

Eh yent often Buh Rabbit ketch at him trick, but eh meet eh match dis time.

Buh Tukrey Buzzud An De Rain

Buh Tukrey Buzzud, him yent hab no sense no how. You watch um. Wen do rain duh po down, eh set on de fench an eh aquinch up isself. Eh draw in eh neck, an eh try fur hide eh head, an eh look dat pittyful you rale sorry for um. Eh duh half cry, an eh say to isself: "Nummine, wen dis rain ober me guine buil house right off. Me yent guine leh dis rain lick me dis way no mo."

Wen de rain done gone, an de win blow, an de sun shine, wuh buh Tukrey Buzzud do? Eh set on de top er de dead pine ree way di sun kin wam um, an eh retch out eh wing, an eh tun roun an roun so de win kin dry eh fedder, an eh laugh to isself, an eh say: "Dis rain done ober. Eh yent guine rain no mo. No use fur me fuh buil house now." Caless man dis like Buh Tukrey Buzzud.

De Eagle An Eh Chillun

De Eagle, him duh er wise bud. Eh mek en nes on one tall pine tree close de ribber, er de sea, way nuttne kin git at um. Eh saterfy wide two chillun.Eh tek good care er um. Ebry hour eh fetch um snake an fish, an eh garde um from win an rain an fowl-hawk, an mek um grow fas. Wen eh wing kibber wid fedder an eh strong nough fur fly, whu Buh Eagle do? Eh wint leff dem chillun een de nes fuh lazy an lib pontopper eh farruh an eh murrer, but eh tek um on eh wing, an eh sail ober de sea, an eh tell eh chillun: "De time come fuh you fuh mek you own libbin. Me feed you long nough. Now you haffer look out fuh youself." Wid dat, eh fly from onder dem, an de noung bud, wen eh fine out eh murrer yent gwine cahr um no furder, an dat dem haffer shif fuh demself, dem rtry eh wing an sail off een de element duh hunt bittle. People orter tek notus er buh Eagle an do jes es him do. Wen you chillun git big nough fuh wuk, mek um wuk. Dont leh um set bout de house duh do nuttne, an duh spek eh farruh an eh murrer fuh fine bittle an cloze fuh um. Ef you does, you chillun gwine mek you shame, an eh will tun out berry triflin. Eh will keep you dead po, too. Do same luk buh Eagle. Mine you chillun well wen dem leetle; an soon dem big nough fuh wuk, mek um wuk.

Buh Roccoon An Buh Possum

Buh Roccoon ax Buh Possum wuh mek, wen de dog tackle um, eh double up ehself, an kibber eh yeye wid eh han, an wunt fight lucker man an lick de dog off. Buh Possom grin eh teet same lucker fool, an eh say, wen de dog come pon topper um, dem tickle him rib so bad long demmout dat him bleege ter laugh; an so him furgit fuh fight.

The Vanishing Gullah/Geechee Culture

After the upheaval of the Civil War and the changes of the Reconstruction era from 1865 through 1877, the sea islands experienced relative stability to the end of the century. Following the demise of rice and cotton cultivation, truck farming and tree farming arose in the area. Despite the migration of African Americans from the fields of the South to the cities of the North, beginning after World War I, the population of the sea islands remained rather staple and overwhelmingly black through the first half  of the twentieth century. Even in the mid-1950s most natives remained on their local island. The building of bridges and roads, beginning in the 1930s, led in time to commuting and erosion of the isolation that had produced a unique culture. Federal projects created more arable land, improved farming practices, and increased productivity, but pushed residents off the land and introduced a cash-based  society. The shift from a barter to a money economy altered the culture and social structure of the Gullah and Geechee people. More profound change followed the purchase of large tracts of land on Hilton Head Island for their timber in 1950. Entrepreneurs began to consolidate cheap land and "tax land" on the sea islands. Through family inheritance everyone had received a small portion of property and relatives who had moved to New York were offered a small cash settlement for their "*heir rights.*" When tax values rose on waterfront property beyond the financial capacity of Gullah and Geechee farmers, a friendly corporation would pay the tax, buy up the land, and force the natives to move. By 1980 whites outnumbered blacks on Hilton Head Island five to one.

Today the Gullah and Geechee people face a crisis today as the demand for their land and marsh encroaches upon home and farm and threatens their way of life. The succeeding years since the 1950's have seen even more rapid change. Although the marsh and the dikes of old rice plantations still persist, the Carolina and Georgia coast is vastly different today from  what it was at the beginning of this century. The public schools discourage the use of the Gullah/Geechee language and teach the goals of a society geared to production and progress rather than the ideal of equilibrium that has long characterized this culture unconcerned with time.

Yet there is hope as natives have become more aware of their rights and opportunities and new organizations seek to preserve their way of life. Saving a culture goes hand in hand with saving an ecology.

Low Country Cooking

DEVILED CRAB

1 lb. crab meat
2 hard-boiled eggs
1 cup diced celery
(cooked slightly)
2 cups medium white sauce **
Salt & Pepper to taste
3 tbs prepared mustard
Cracker crumbs

Combine crab meat, boiled eggs (diced) and celery. Mix with white sauce and mustard. Fill crab backs and sprinkle with cracker crums and dot each with butter. Bake at 400 degrees for 30 minutes.

White Sauce: 2 Tablespoons butter; 1 cup milk; 2 tablespoons all-purpose flour. In a small sauce pan over medium heat, melt butter. Add flour and stir until the butter and flour are well combined. Pour in milk, stirring constantly as it thickens. Add more milk depending on desired consistency.

SHRIMP CURRY

4 tablespoons butter
3 pounds Shrimp, boiled and cleaned
1 large onion chopped fine
2 tablespoons curry powder
1/2 cup apple chopped fine
1/2 cup celery chopped fine
1-1/2 cups water
1 pint cream
Salt and Pepper to taste

Put butter in a frying pan. When melted, add onion, apple and celery. Simmer these, then add water. Let all simmer gently until apple and celery are tender and most of the liquid has cooked away. Stir into the mixture the seasonings. Add the cream and Shrimp. Cook gently until cream is reduced to sauce consistency. Serve with plenty of well-cooked rice. Have small bowls of grated coconut, chutney, chopped almonds and pickle relish. Serves 6-8.

FRIED SHRIMP

1 pound raw Shrimp
2 eggs
2 tablespoons milk or water
Cracker meal
Fat for Frying
Salt and pepper

Remove the heads and peel shrimp, leaving last segment and tail on. Dip each shrimp in egg which has been beaten and mixed with milk and water. Roll in cracker crumbs to which salt and pepper have been added. Fry in hot deep fat until golden brown. Drain and serve hot with cocktail sauce.

CRAB STEW

1 lb. Crab meat
2 cups half & half
1/4 teaspoon graded lemon peel
1/2 stick of butter
1/2 cup cracker crumbs
1 to 2 tablespoons of Sherry

Put butter, milk, mace and graded lemon in top of double-boiler. Allow to simmer for a few minutes until butter is fully melted and then add cracker crumbs and salt and pepper to taste. Cook slowly for 15 minutes. Add sherry just before serving.

RED RICE

2 Cups Rice
1 can Tomato paste
1-2 cans water
2 onions (chopped fine)
3 teaspoons salt
2-3 teaspoons sugar
4 strips bacon (Need 1/2 pound of bacon)
8 tablespoons bacon grease
good dash of pepper

Fry bacon and remove from pan. Saute' onions in bacon grease. Add tomato paste, water, salt, sugar and pepper. Cook uncovered slowly (about 10 minutes) until mixture measures 2 cups and then add it to rice in top section of steamer. Add the 1/2 cup additional grease. Steam for 1/2 hour and then add Bacon, crumbled and stir with a fork. Cook 30-45 minutes longer. Serves 6-8.

CRAB SOUP

1 can cream of Tomato soup
1 can bouillon
1 cup sherry
1 can green pea soup
1 cup coffee cream
Crabmeat to suit (little less than 1 lb.)

Heat together adding sherry after heated.
Serve with chopped parsley and slice of
lemon.

FRIED OYSTERS

1 quart oysters
2 eggs beaten
2 tablespoons milk
Salt and pepper
1 cup bread crumbs or corn meal

Drain oysters. Mix eggs, milk and seasonings. Dip oysters in egg mixture and roll in crumbs. Fry in deep fat (375 degrees) about 2 minutes or until brown. Or fry in shallow fat about 2 minutes on one side, turn and brown on other side. Serves 6.

BISCUITS

1 cup all purpose flour
1 heaping teaspoon baking powder
1/2 teaspoon salt
2 heaping tablespoons shortening
1/2 cup milk

Sift flour and then measure. Add baking powder and salt and sift into bowl. Cut in shortening with a fork until fine meal. Add milk slowly until right consistency and not too sticky. Take a good forkful of dough and roll between floured hands quickly to oblong shape two inches long. Prick with fork. Put on ungreased sheet in oven and bake at 500 degrees for 12 to 15 minutes. Makes a dozen biscuits that will melt in your mouth.

SHRIMP PILAU

1 lb. raw Shrimp
4 slices Bacon
1 cup raw rice
1/2 cup minced celery
1 medium Onion, sliced finely
1 cup water
Salt to taste

Peel raw Shrimp. Cut up Bacon and brown with celery and onion. Add Shrimp and cook without cover for 5 minutes. Add water and rice. Let come to good boil for 7 minutes. Reduce heat as low as possible. Cover and continue to cook for about 14 minutes or until Rice is done.

SHRIMP & GRITS

Put ingredients below in a frying pan and
heat:

3 tablespoons Wesson Oil
1 tablespoon Vinegar
1 tablespoon Worcestershire Sauce
1 tablespoon Butter
Pinch of Salt and Pepper and dry Mustard

Add: 1 qt. cooked, devined Shrimp *(use
small Shrimp from Creek or River)*. Heat
thoroughly and then serve with Grits for
Breakfast.

OYSTER STEW

1 Pint Oysters
1 Pint Milk
Butter, Salt & Pepper to taste
2 Tablespoons finely diced Onion

Bring Oysters to boil in their own juice until puffy. Lightly saute Onion in butter being careful not to brown. In saucepan bring Milk, butter, salt and pepper to a scald being sure not to boil. Drop in Oysters and Onion and heat thoroughly. Add Sherry wine to taste. Makes 2-3 servings.

Gullah Cooking-Related Terms

Aig - egg

Aipun - apron

Ash cake – cornbread wrapped in a damp towel and baked in the ashes of a fire

Ashish - ashes

Bakien – bacon

Barruh - a male hog that has been castrated before being slaughtered for its meat

Benne – sesame seeds. The seeds were made into cookies and candies and were believed to bring good luck. The seeds had arrived with the slaves in necklaces and were planted near the cabins or in the gardens.

Bile – to boil

Bittle – foods

Bryaberry - blackberry

Brekwus – breakfast

Brunswick stew – a mixture of corn, tomatoes, onions, rice, lima beans, potatoes, and chicken, pork, ground beef, and/or squirrel and other small game. The term "Brunswick stew" was not used widely in the Gullah region until the late nineteenth century. Food historians disagree as to the name's origin, but most Georgians are convinced it originated in Brunswick, on the Georgia coast. A big iron wash pot and plaque in Brunswick, Georgia commemorate the first batch supposedly ever made.

Buckruhbittle - food eaten by whites

Cawch - to scorch

Cawn – corn

Cawn puddin' – a baked mixture of creamed corn, cornmeal, and eggs

Cawnmeal dumplins – cornmeal and water dropped by spoonfuls into boiling greens

Chiney - glass or china plates, cups, and saucers

Chitlins – pig intestines

Chitlins and maw – pig intestines and stomach boiled, cut into small pieces, and seasoned with the trinity and hot peppers

Chow chow – a sweet, hot relish made of vegetables, peppers, vinegar, and sugar. This was a way to use and preserve late-season vegetables that might remain in the garden. When there weren't enough of one type for a "mess," the odds and ends were harvested for chow chow. The first mention of "chow chow" relish was in an eighteenth-century South Carolina cookbook. It was often eaten with dried beans and cornbread.

Clabbuh – curdled milk with a yogurt-like taste and texture

Coota – a soft-shell turtle that was often made into a soup

Corn fritters – fresh corn, cornmeal, and egg, dropped by spoonfuls into hot fat

Cracklins – crisp bits of fried pork skin

Crackuh salad - stale crackers, tomatoes, onions, mayonnaise, and seasonings

Cyasnet - cast net

116

Dub - dove

Fannuh - a shallow basket woven of grass, used for winnowing rice

Fiyah - fire

Flaybuh - to add seasonings to a dish

Feeduhm - to serve a meal

Frogmore stew – shrimp, sausage, corn-on-the-cob, spices, and potatoes, all boiled together. Sometimes crabs and clams were included.

Frybakien - fried bacon

Fufu – pounded yams mixed with egg and onions, often served with stews or roasted meat

Gatuh etouffe - strips of alligator meat, butter, flour, the trinity, and stewed tomatoes

Goobers – peanuts

Greece - to add lard to a pan

Grunnuts - peanuts

Gullah rice – rice, sausage, chopped chicken livers, and the trinity

Gumbo – a thick stew of okra, the trinity, shrimp, sausage, chicken, and/or ham

Gyaadn - garden

Hahbis - harvest

Hibe - beehive

Hobo bread – flour, eggs, lard, raisins, nuts, sugar, and boiling water, baked in a loaf pan.

117

boiling water, baked in a loaf pan

Hoe cake – a bread made of salt, cornmeal, and water, traditionally cooked on a greased hoe over an open fire

Hog maw – the stomach of a pig

Hom'ny - hominy

Hongry - hungry

Hoppin' John – rice, black-eyed peas, ham, onions, cayenne, and bacon grease

Hull pie – a pie made of grape skins

Hush puppies – a mixture of cornmeal, buttermilk, egg, and onions, fried in hot fat

Jumble cakes – small sweet cakes. The dough was rolled into small ropes and formed into circles, then baked.

Kush – cornbread cooked on a griddle and topped with raw onions and ham gravy

Lahd - lard

Lassis cake – cake sweetened with molasses instead of sugar

Limpin' Susan – shrimp and rice flavored with bell peppers and onions

Muhlassis – molasses

Mustud grins - mustard greens

Mynaze - what the Gullah descendants call mayonnaise

Nyam – eats, eating, ate

Onion pie – onions, cheese, cream, and eggs baked in a pie crust

Osituh – oyster

Peanut chop – a chicken stew flavored with tomatoes, hot peppers, and peanuts

Pilau – rice with salted fish, pork, or wild game

Pinduh – peanuts

Possimmun - persimmon

Pot likker – the liquid left over from a pot of greens. This was "sopped" with cornbread.

Purloo – a mixture of bacon, onion, okra, ham, tomatoes, rice, and herbs

Rashin - rations

Red rice – rice cooked with bacon, onions, and tomatoes

Rice bread – a heavy bread made from ground rice

Rokkoon - raccoon

Roostah pie - the stewed flesh of an older chicken baked in a pie crust with vegetables

Seafood muddle – a stew of fish stock, onions, celery, garlic, tomatoes, potatoes, fish, clams, shrimp, and mussels

Shahk - shark meat

She-crab soup – a rich mixture of blue crabmeat, crab roe, cream, butter, and spices

Shrimp bog – bacon, shrimp, rice, tomatoes, and chicken broth

Suppuh - the evening meal

119

Supshun – any food that is especially nutritional and tasty

Squirrel burgoo – a stew of squirrel meat, beans, okra, and cornmeal

Sweet bread – bread made from wheat flour

Sweetnin' - sugar, molasses, honey, and cane syrup

Sweet tada pone – sweet potatoes, cane syrup, eggs, butter, and nutmeg

Swimp 'n' grits – stewed shrimp, pork fat, and gravy, served over grits

Swit - delicious

Tadas - potatoes

Talluh - beef fat

Tase - taste

Tuckrey – turkey

Tuhnflour – cornmeal mush or porridge

Tunnup - turnip

Watermillion - watermelon

Wegitubble – vegetable

Wine - vine

Wineguh - vinegar

Yalluh yam - a sweet potato with yellow flesh

Yams – sweet potatoes

About The Author

Pearce W. Hammond was born and raised in Savannah, Georgia is an accomplished writer, artist and photographer. In his youth he spent a lot of time on the coastal waters of the low country and attributes his interest in writing and art to his famed Savannah-born uncle, Johnny Mercer, who  wrote over 1,000 songs and won four Academy Awards. When not writing songs, Johnny Mercer was also a talented painter and could speak and understand the Gullah/Geechee language which fascinated the young Hammond.

The author has written several other books that include a humorous book about dogs; a humorous book about old age and senior moments; a humorous book about frequent flying; and a book on the Gullahs of South Carolina which is illustrated with his original paintings. His art has been featured in many local and regional publications.

He and his wife, Anne, now reside on the tidal waters of the Chechessee River in Okatie, South Carolina.

Other Books by
Pearce W. Hammond

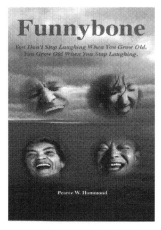

"Funnybone"

This book contains wild and witty quotes about old ag
Hilarious examples of senior moments; Funny jokes abo
age and aging; and much, much more!

*"Sometimes I can't remember what I did yesterday but I co
still remember many of the jokes which were told to n
over the years. I hope this book tickles your Funnybone an
make you laugh because laughter is needed in this cra
world we live in today."*
                                    Pearce W. Hammond, Author

Paperback 2012   ISBN 9781480034624

Available Online From:
www.amazon.com
www.pearcehammond.com
https://www.createspace.com/4014853

Other Books by Pearce W. Hammond

"Listen To Me"

This book gives a humorous glimpse into the lives of dogs from their point-of-view and answers many of the questions that have been *"dogging"* humans for years, such as: Can dogs write poetry? Do dogs have wisdom? What do dogs think about during the day? Can people learn from dogs, and much, much more. This book is a must-read for every dog owner and dog lover who wants to experience the therapeutic effects of laughing.

Paperback 2011   ISBN 9781461132790

Available Online From:

www.amazon.com
www.pearcehammond.com
https://www.createspace.com/3604066

Other Books by Pearce W. Hammond

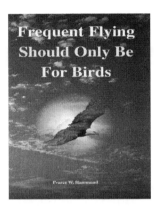

"Frequent Flying Should Only Be For Birds "

If you are a Frequent Flyer or an In-Frequent Flyer, this humorous book about flying is for you. The author spent many hours in the air as a Frequent Flyer and earned the right to write this book which contains humorous chapters on: You know you're a frequent flyer when....; Frequent Flyer Dictionary; Quotes about flying; Airway Rules; Airline Obituaries; Flight Attendant Humor; and Flying Jokes.

Paperback   2013   ISBN 9781482004229

Available Online From:
www.amazon.com
www.pearcehammond.com
https://www.createspace.com/4135847

Other Books by Pearce W. Hammond

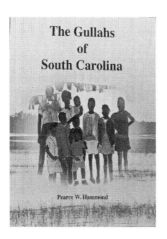

"The Gullahs of South Carolina"

This book tells an important story about the Gullah people of South Carolina and their vanishing way of life and culture. It is illustrated with the author's colorful original paintings and creates public awareness of the Gullahs unique language, lifestyle and culture so that future generations will know and recognize the significant contributions the Gullah people of South Carolina have made to America's heritage.

Paperback   2011   ISBN 9780615486482

Available Online From:

www.amazon.com
www.pearcehammond.com
https://www.createspace.com/3605666

Bibliography

Branch, Muriel M. *The Water Brought us*. New York, NY: Cobblehill Books, 1995.

Conroy, Pat. *The Water is Wide*. Boston, MA: Houghton Mifflin, 1972.

Jones, Charles C., Jr. *Negro Myths from the Georgia Coast,* Told in the Vernacular. Boston: Houghton, Mifflin,1888.

Geraty, Virginia M., *Gullah For You*. Orangeburg, SC: Sandlapper Publishing Co. Inc., 1997.

McFeely, William S. *Sapelo's People*. New York, NY: W.W. Norton & Co., Inc., 1994.

Pollitzer, William S. *The Gullah People and Their African Heritage*. Athens, GA: University of Georgia Press, 1999.

Carawan, Guy and Candie. *Ain't you got a right to the tree of life?* Athens, GA: The University of Georgia Press, 1989.

Turner, Lorenzo D. *Africanisms in the Gullah Dialect*. Columbia, SC.: University of South Carolina Press, 1969.

Chase, Judith W. *Afro-American Art and Craft*. New York: Van Nostrand, 1971.

Jones, Katherine M. *Port Royal Under Six Flags*.
Indianapolis: Bobbs-Merrill, 1960.

Gullah lyrics To Carolina Low Country Spirituals.
Charleston, SC: Society for the Preservation of
Spirituals, 2007.

Kovacik, Charles F. *South Carolina: A Geography*.
Boulder, CO: Westview Press, 1987.

Parrish, Lydia. *Slave Songs of the Georgia Sea Islands*.
Athens, GA: University of Georgia Press, 1992.

Woofter, T.J. Black Yeomanry: *Life on St. Helena
Island*. New York: Henry Holt, 1930.

Joyner, Charles W. *Down by the Riverside*. Urbanna:
University of Illinois Press, 1984.

Hamilton, Virginia. *The People Could Fly: American
Black Folktales*. New York: Knopf, 1985.

Donald, Henderson. *The Negro Freedman*. New York:
H. Schuman, 1952.

Smith, Julia F. *Slavery and Rice Culture in Lowcountry
Georgia, 1750-1860*. Knoxville: University of
Tennessee Press, 1985.

Parsons, Elsie Clewes. *Folklore of the Sea Islands*.
Cambridge, MA: American Folklore Society, 1923.

Notes

Notes

Notes

Made in the USA
Lexington, KY
15 August 2014